LEARN
TO RIDE

Written by Sandy Ransford

The publisher would like to thank the following for their
kind permission to reproduce their photographs:
Ray Moller and Peter Chadwick
Illustrations: Pete Serjeant

A Funfax Book
First published in Great Britain by Funfax Ltd.,
an imprint of Dorling Kindersley Limited,
9 Henrietta Street, London WC2E 8PS
Copyright © 1999 Funfax Ltd.

CHOOSING A SCHOOL

This book will guide you through some of the things you need to know about learning to ride, but you must also seek expert instruction. A national riding association, such as the British Horse Society, will be able to provide you with a list of approved riding schools in your area.

Stables

Look for well-maintained stables and a tidy yard without bits of hay and straw blowing around.

What to Look For

Go and look at each school before you choose one. A good riding school will look clean and tidy. The ponies will be well fed and contented, and their tack (saddles and bridles) will be clean and supple. The fields will be properly fenced, and not overstocked with ponies, grazed down to the ground or covered in droppings and clumps of weeds. The staff will have proper qualifications, and be pleasant and friendly. All the riders will be wearing hard hats. Schools will often lend you one that fits if you don't have one of your own.

Indoor School

An indoor school is useful for winter riding.

WHAT TO WEAR

The most important piece of riding kit is a hard hat, to protect your head in case of a fall.

> **Hat**
> Your hat may be either a crash helmet without a peak, or a velvet-covered hard hat with a peak. It should have special straps to hold it in place, and it must fit properly.

This young rider is wearing a crash helmet which shades her eyes from the sun and rain. It is covered with a 'silk'.

Boots
On your feet you can wear ankle-high jodhpur boots, or knee-length rubber or leather boots.

Other Clothing
Special jodhpurs, or 'breeches', which have padding over the inside of your knees, are more comfortable to wear than ordinary trousers, although they aren't essential to start with. Avoid wearing jeans with thick inner seams, as they will rub your legs. A loose-fitting T-shirt or sweatshirt is an ideal top. For cold or wet weather you will need a water-proof jacket and special riding gloves, which have surfaces designed not to slip on the reins.

This young rider's long hair is tied back neatly. The padding on her jodhpurs protects her legs from rubbing on the saddle; her jodhpur boots protect her ankles from the stirrups.

HORSE SENSE

By 'horse sense' we mean understanding a horse's or pony's behaviour. This helps us to know how to handle him.

Handling Ponies

Although they are large and strong, horses and ponies are nervous animals. We get them to do what we want by calm (and sometimes determined!) persuasion, but never by force, rough handling or shouting at them.

Approach a pony quietly and calmly, then he will trust you. Don't make a lot of noise, or run around. If you feel nervous, your pony will sense it and feel nervous, too. Talk to him, and give him a pat on the neck. A calm, confident pony will have his ears pricked forward. If his ears are back, especially if they are flattened back, he's unhappy about something. Keep your feet away from his, and if you walk behind him, run your hand round his hindquarters and down on to his tail, so that he knows where you are.

When you give a pony a titbit, hold your hand out flat and keep your fingers together.

CATCHING AND LEADING

LEARN TO RIDE

You may have to catch your pony before you can ride him. Take an apple or a carrot with you, and hold the headcollar behind your back.

Approaching and Catching

Approach the pony from the front, so that he can see you, and hold out the titbit (see opposite page). As he stretches out his neck to take the titbit, slip the headcollar rope around his neck. Then, standing on the pony's left-hand side, put the noseband over his nose. Reach under his jaw with your right hand to pass the headpiece of the headcollar over the top of his head. Catch hold of it with your left hand and do up the buckle. Give the pony a pat and another titbit.

Leading

To lead him, hold the rope with your right hand up by the headcollar and your left hand near the end of the rope. Don't forget to close the gate behind you.

Walk straight ahead when leading a pony, don't look back at him.

TACK

Tack is the saddle and bridle, and any other equipment a pony wears when you are riding him.

Bridle
The bridle is a collection of straps which hold the bit in the pony's mouth and enable you to control him.

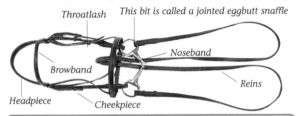

Throatlash *This bit is called a jointed eggbutt snaffle*

Noseband

Browband

Reins

Headpiece *Cheekpiece*

Saddle
The saddle makes riding more comfortable for both you and your pony. It is held in place by a girth around the pony's tummy, and has stirrups and stirrup irons to help you get on and off, and keep you secure. The saddle may have a pad called a 'numnah' underneath it. Tack is usually made of leather, and has to be cleaned and saddle-soaped to keep it in good condition.

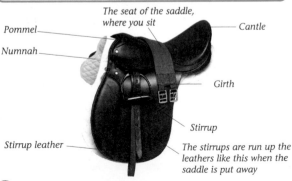

The seat of the saddle, where you sit

Pommel

Cantle

Numnah

Girth

Stirrup

Stirrup leather

The stirrups are run up the leathers like this when the saddle is put away

TACKING UP

Putting on a saddle and bridle is called 'tacking up'. Until you have done this a few times, make sure that an experienced person checks your pony's tack before you ride.

Putting on the Bridle
To put on the bridle, first lift the reins over the pony's head. Then hold the bridle as shown in the picture. Press the bit against the pony's teeth and slip it into his mouth. Slip the headpiece over the top of his head, then fasten the throatlash and the noseband.

Space to Move
You should be able to get your fist between the pony's jaw and the throatlash, and two fingers between his jaw and the noseband.

Putting on the Saddle
Standing on the pony's left side, hold the saddle further forwards than it should sit, then slide it back into position. From the other side, let the girth down and make sure that it isn't twisted. Go back to the left side, reach under the pony for the end of the girth and fasten the buckles. Smooth out the pony's skin after you have tightened the girth.

Buckle the girth on to the front two straps or the front and back straps.

MOUNTING

Mounting means getting on the pony. Before you do, you must check that the pony's girth is tight. To get your stirrups about the right length, adjust the leather so that when you stretch it out under your arm, the iron reaches your armpit while your fingertips are touching the buckle.

The Correct Position

Stand on the pony's left side, facing its tail. Hold the reins in your left hand and with your right hand get hold of the back part of the stirrup iron

and turn it towards you. Put your left foot in the stirrup, catch hold of the saddle with your right hand and spring upwards off your right foot.

Swing Your Leg

Swing your right leg over the pony's back, taking care not to kick him, and lower yourself gently into the saddle. Feel for the right stirrup, turn the front of it away from the pony, and put your right foot in it.

DISMOUNTING

Dismounting means getting off the pony. The idea is to land safely on both feet, while still keeping hold of the reins and being in control of the pony.

The Right Way
Take both feet out of the stirrups. Hold the reins in your left hand and rest your right hand on the front of the saddle. Lean forwards and swing your right leg over the pony's back, again being careful not to kick him. Drop gently down to the ground, landing by the pony's shoulder.

> **The Wrong Way**
> Never try to dismount by swinging your right leg over the front of the saddle. You would have to let go of the reins, and if the pony walks on you could fall over backwards.

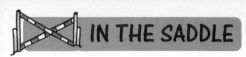 # IN THE SADDLE

The first time you sit on a pony, it will probably feel quite strange, but don't worry. For your first riding lesson you are likely to be on a leading rein, led by an instructor. There will be a strap around the pony's neck for you to hold on to, so that you don't pull on the reins.

How to Sit

Sit in the deepest part of the saddle, with your back straight and your head up. Look ahead, not down at the pony. Let your legs hang down naturally by his sides, then draw your lower legs back slightly. You are sitting in the correct position if an imaginary vertical line would pass through your ear, shoulder, hip and heel. Rest the balls of your feet in the stirrups, and press your heels down. You may need to adjust the length of the leathers slightly until you get into a comfortable position.

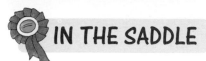

IN THE SADDLE

How to Hold the Reins

Take hold of the reins, and make sure that they are not twisted. Pass them between your

third and fourth fingers and up through your hands, resting your thumbs on the top of them. Your hands should be a few centimetres apart.

Just Relax

Let your arms hang down by your sides and keep your elbows close to your body. Your elbows should be bent at right angles, so that your forearms form straight lines from your elbows and along the reins to the pony's mouth. You should be able to feel his mouth, but you shouldn't pull at it. There are so many things to think about once you are in the saddle that it's easy to sit very stiffly, but try to relax. Once your pony is walking on, your whole body should follow his movements.

WALK ON

Walking is the pony's slowest pace, and his feet
hit the ground one after the other: one, two,
three, four. You control your pony through a
series of instructions, called 'aids'. Your hands,
legs, body movements, voice and whip are all
aids, although you won't use the whip until
you are more experienced.

First Steps

Before you tell your pony to walk on, make sure
that you are sitting correctly. Your legs should be
held close to the pony's sides, you should be able
to feel his mouth through the reins and bit, and
you should be sitting up straight. To give the aids
for walk, make a little more contact with the reins,
press your lower legs firmly against the pony's
sides, and push your bottom down into the saddle.
As he starts to move forwards, relax your hold on
the reins, but still keep contact.

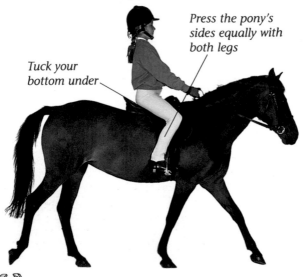

*Press the pony's
sides equally with
both legs*

*Tuck your
bottom under*

LEARN TO RIDE

WALK ON

Move With the Pony

Let your body relax and move with the pony. As he walks, he will nod his head up and down and you must relax your hands a little at each movement to allow him to do so. Once the pony is walking, you can relax your leg aid, unless he is lazy and wants to stop, in which case you will need to keep your legs pressed against his sides.

LEARN TO RIDE

Halting

To halt, take a firm hold of the reins and close your legs against the pony's sides. You are driving him forwards into his bit with your legs, but not allowing him to move forwards with your hands, so he stops. As soon as he does so, relax your legs and hands, and give him a pat. When you get more experienced you will be able to bring your pony to a four-square halt, with his forelegs and hindlegs perfectly in line.

TURNING LEFT

Once you can walk forward and halt, you need to be able to change direction. A lot of work in the riding school involves riding in circles and going the opposite way round – 'changing the rein'. The picture below shows how a pony's whole body curves round in the direction you are going when you turn.

Turning Left

To turn left, pull slightly on the left rein, and let your right hand move forwards to follow the direction of the pony's head. Press your inside (left) leg into his side to keep him moving forwards. Bring your outside (right) leg back behind the girth to stop the pony's hindquarters from swinging out to the right. Turn your own head and body towards the left and look in the direction you are going.

To turn left, the rider pulls gently on the left rein and gives with the right hand.

Looking down from above shows how the pony's body bends when turning, and how the rider adjusts her position.

LEARN TO RIDE

Turning Right

To turn to the right, you reverse the aids. Pull gently on the right rein, let the left hand move forwards, press with your right leg to keep the pony moving forwards and bring your left leg back behind the girth to stop the pony's quarters swinging out to the left.

Back into Position

As soon as you have made your turn, move your hands and legs back to the normal position. Press with both legs to keep the pony moving fowards, and maintain contact with the reins. If you are riding a circle, you need to keep your hands, legs and body in the position for the turn to a greater or lesser extent, depending on the size of the circle.

LEARN TO RIDE

When turning right, the rider's left leg is held behind the girth.

TROTTING

The trot is the next pace up from the walk. The pony's legs move in diagonal pairs: near (left) front and off (right) hind together; off front and near hind together. Because of this, trotting feels very bumpy until you get used to it.

Rising Trot

To make trotting more comfortable, you will be taught to rise to the trot. This means that you sit in the saddle while one pair of feet hits the ground, and rise a little way out of it when the opposite pair does. When you first try this, it will seem very difficult, then one day you'll get the hang of it and find it very easy. Practise rising out of the saddle with the pony standing still. Take your weight on the stirrups, and push your heels down. Then sit down again. Try going up and down in the rhythm of the trot: one, two, one, two. You can also practise while the pony is walking.

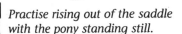

Practise rising out of the saddle with the pony standing still.

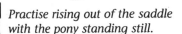

Sitting Trot

Although you will use rising trot when out for a ride, you need to learn to sit to the trot if you want to progress with your riding. You also need to be able to do it before you learn to canter. The idea is to sit down in the saddle as deeply as you can, keeping your bottom in contact with it throughout the up-and-down movements. It's not easy. It takes a lot of practice, and some ponies are more comfortable than others. Try to relax and let your body absorb the motion. If you feel insecure, hold on to the pommel (front) of the saddle, or a neckstrap, if your pony is wearing one. Once you can do sitting trot with your feet in the stirrups, your instructor will probably ask you to cross your stirrups over in front of the saddle and do it without them.

LEARN TO RIDE

The bandages on the pony's legs show how they move in diagonal pairs when trotting. On the left the rider is doing rising trot; on the right, sitting trot.

Once you have learned the basics, you can then have lessons on the lunge. A lunge rein is a long rein attached to the pony by a special noseband called a 'cavesson'. Side reins go from the pony's bit to the girth straps to help control him, and you ride without reins.

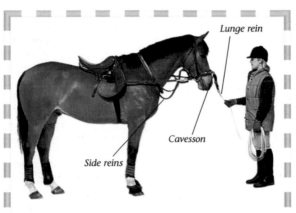

Lunge rein

Cavesson

Side reins

A horse prepared for a lunge lesson. The rein is about 10 m/33 ft long.

First Lessons

You may hold on to a neckstrap or to the front of the saddle. The instructor holds the other end of the lunge. He or she will tell the pony to walk or trot in a large circle while you carry out various exercises. Only quiet, sensible ponies are used for these kinds of lessons. Because you don't have to think about controlling your pony, and can concentrate on the way you are sitting, riding on the lunge improves your balance and gives you a better seat.

LEARN TO RIDE

Riding
Without Stirrups

When you first start lessons on the lunge you will have your feet in the stirrups, but when you become more confident you will learn how to ride without them. Sitting on a pony without stirrups helps you to sit right down in the saddle. You can stretch your legs, keeping your heels down and pushing towards the ground. Your body will move more easily to the pony's motion, and your balance will improve. Trotting without stirrups isn't easy at first, and you may feel as if you will bounce off. Hold on to the neckstrap or the front of the saddle until you feel safe.

Exercises
on the Lunge

With your feet back in the stirrups, you can try exercises like those shown here: twisting your body around with your hands on your hips, rolling your head around, and circling your arms.

EXERCISES IN THE SADDLE

These exercises will help your confidence, so that you soon feel as much at home on a pony as you do on the ground. If you are confident and relaxed, your pony will be so, too, and your riding will benefit. Don't try these exercises unless there is an instructor to hold your pony.

Leaning Back

Knot your reins, fold your arms across your chest and, keeping your feet in the stirrups, lean back until you rest your head on the pony's back. Rest for a few moments, then sit up again.

Leaning Forwards

Hold the reins in one hand. Keep your feet and legs in the correct position and lean forwards to touch the pony's forelock with one hand. Go back and repeat the exercise with the other hand.

Toe Touching

Knot your reins. Sit up straight, then lift your right arm up in the air and bring it across your body and reach down to touch your left toe. Try to keep your legs in the corrrect position. Straighten up, then do the exercise with your left arm.

EXERCISES IN THE SADDLE

Round the World

Let go of the reins and take both feet out of the stirrups. Hold the front of the saddle with your right hand, and the back with your left hand. Swing your right leg over the 'pommel' (front of the saddle) so you are sitting side-saddle. Adjust the position of your hands as you move so you always have one hand on the saddle.

And Back Again

Swing your left leg over the 'cantle' (back of the saddle). You will now be facing the pony's tail. Swing your right leg over, so you are facing the opposite side, then swing your left leg over the pommel so you are facing the front again. Take care not to kick your pony when you are doing this exercise, and move slowly and carefully so you don't upset him.

LEARN TO RIDE

CANTERING

Once you are confident, and can sit well down in the saddle, you are ready to canter. The canter is a three-time pace, and a pony leads with either the right or left leg. It has a lovely rocking motion, and you should keep your bottom in the saddle and sit without bouncing. In order to do this you have to relax the lower part of your back.

Trot to Canter

Go into sitting trot, and keep contact with the pony's mouth. To strike off with the left leg leading, keep your left leg on the girth and your right leg a little behind it, and squeeze the pony's sides. You will feel a little hop as he goes into canter. Keep contact with the reins, but let your hands follow the movement of the pony's head and neck. To canter with the right leg leading, reverse your aids.

On a circle the pony should lead with the inside leg. Here the right leg is leading.

GALLOPING

The gallop is like a very fast canter, but it is a four-beat pace. Ponies get very excited when they gallop, so you should only try it when you are confident cantering. You need space in which to gallop, and it's a good idea to go uphill, as the pony will slow down when he gets out of breath!

How to Gallop

Go into the 'forward position', which is the seat you also use for jumping. Shorten your stirrups a hole or two and lean forwards, so that your seat is out of the saddle. Shorten your reins, and take your weight on your knees and feet, with your heels well down. Get your pony into a fairly fast, but controlled canter, then urge him on by squeezing with your legs and relaxing the reins a little. Once he is galloping, maintain contact through the reins. Never gallop past other riders, loose ponies, other animals or walkers, or on a road.

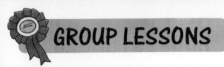

GROUP LESSONS

When you can control your pony, you may join with other riders in a group lesson. This will teach you how to handle a pony in the company of others.

The pony at the back, which is smaller than the others, is having to trot to catch up.

Riding in a Group

Never ride your pony too close to another. Many ponies do not like someone coming up behind them and may kick out, so allow a pony's length between you when following someone else. When passing another rider, either overtaking them or going in the opposite direction, allow at least 1.5 m (5 ft) between the ponies.

Keeping Pace

The person at the front of a string of riders is called the 'leading file', and he or she sets the pace. Try to keep at that pace, and maintain the distance between you and the pony in front. The leading file may be asked to trot on, while the rest keep walking. Be prepared for your pony to want to follow, but make sure that he does what you want him to.

GROUP LESSONS

Exercises in the School

Your group lessons will take place in an indoor or outdoor school with letter markers around the edge, as shown in the diagram. You may be asked to walk from A to E, trot to M, then change the rein (go in the opposite direction) from M to K, then trot to F, for example. Or you may be asked to walk or trot a 10 m (11 yds) diameter circle, or a 20 m (22 yds) one. Riding a figure-of-eight is a good test of your ability. You should make both halves of the eight the same size and, of course, you have to ride first in one direction and then in the other. Several riders may be asked to carry out exercises at the same time, or you may line up and take it in turn. This way you can see how other people perform, and learn from their mistakes.

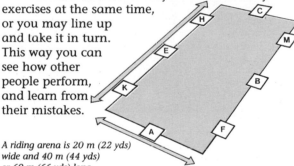

A riding arena is 20 m (22 yds) wide and 40 m (44 yds) or 60 m (66 yds) long.

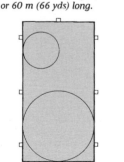

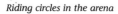

Riding circles in the arena

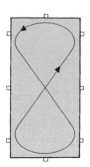

Riding a figure-of-eight

GOING FOR A RIDE

Riding out in the countryside, or 'hacking', is great fun. Your pony may be more excitable out on a ride with others, so try to keep him calm. When you first go out hacking, go with an experienced rider, and tell an adult where you are going.

In the Country
You may ride along bridlepaths, through woods, or have to cross boggy ground or even a shallow stream. Be prepared for the unexpected, and try to anticipate problems. For example, if you are riding under trees, you need to watch out for exposed roots and holes that your pony may trip over, and duck to avoid low branches. If your bridlepath crosses a field, watch out for livestock. They may all come charging up to inspect you, which will upset your pony.

Country Ride

Walk the first mile out, to warm up your pony's muscles, and the last mile home, to cool him off. In between you can have a trot and a canter if the ground is suitable – that means smooth and level, not deeply rutted or boggy. Only canter where it is fairly soft. Cantering over ground baked hard by the summer sun may harm your pony's legs.

Dos and Don'ts

- Don't ride across private land unless you have the owner's permission.
- Ride around the edges of fields, rather than across the centre.
- Go slowly where there are animals in fields, or if you meet other riders or walkers.
- Don't overtake another rider without asking their permission. If you have to open any gates, be sure to close them behind you.

Don't ride through water unless you know it is shallow and has a firm footing.

RIDING ON THE ROAD

Don't ride out on a road unless you are sure that you can control your pony in all situations and know about the traffic regulations. It is best to go in a group with your instructor at first.

Road Sense

Keep to the left and if possible ride on the verge, but look out for ditches. Always be aware of what is happening around you. Some drivers are very impatient, so don't assume they will slow down or wait for you. On a narrow road, pull into a gateway to let cars pass. If you are overtaking a parked car, check behind you before riding around it, and give it a wide berth if someone is in it. The driver may open the door or start the engine.

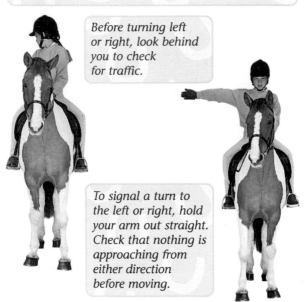

Before turning left or right, look behind you to check for traffic.

To signal a turn to the left or right, hold your arm out straight. Check that nothing is approaching from either direction before moving.

RIDING ON THE ROAD

Be Polite

It is important to be polite to other road users. Walk past pedestrians and raise your hand to thank drivers who slow down when passing you. If you are worried about taking your hand off the rein, nod and smile instead. If a driver waits behind you, wave him on when it is safe to overtake, that is if no traffic is approaching from the opposite direction, your pony is not nervous, and there is room for him to do so.

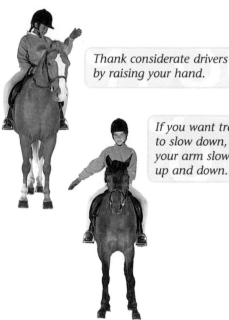

Thank considerate drivers by raising your hand.

If you want traffic to slow down, wave your arm slowly up and down.

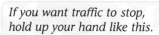

If you want traffic to stop, hold up your hand like this.

LEARN TO RIDE

LEARNING TO JUMP

Jumping is not too difficult once you have learned how to balance, which comes with practice.

Forward Position

Before starting to jump, you need to learn the forward position. Try it first with your pony standing still. Shorten both stirrups a hole or two, shorten your reins, then lean forward with your bottom just clear of the saddle. Take your weight on the balls of your feet in the stirrups, and keep your heels down. Keep your head up and look ahead.

Trotting Poles

Your first lessons will probably be over trotting poles. This gives you the chance to practise the forward position. Try to absorb the bumpiness in your back, knees and ankles. If you feel wobbly, hold on to a neckstrap – don't pull on the reins.

Leading Rein

You may learn to jump on a leading rein, with an adult running beside you.

This young rider would be better balanced if his hands were lower and his heels were down.

Taking a Jump

From trotting poles you will progress to taking small jumps. Let your hands go forwards to allow the pony to stretch his neck as he jumps. Take care not to pull on his mouth as you land.

LEARN TO RIDE

SHOWS AND GYMKHANAS

Before you go to a
show, make sure
that your pony is
well groomed; clean
his tack thoroughly
and check that
your own clothes
are smart. If you
have to transport
your pony, make
sure that he will
load, and allow
plenty of time.

Polish Your Skills

Whether you are entered in showing, jumping
or gymkhana classes, spend a few weeks
practising before the show. In showjumping,
you must concentrate hard all the way round.
Gymkhana events are a good test of your skill
and control.

At the Show

When you arrive at the
showground, collect your
numbers and make sure
that you know where you
are meant to be and what
time your class is. Look
after your pony. Don't
tear around on him all
day. Give him a rest, in
the shade if it is hot.
Take his bridle off and
let him graze, and make
sure that he has water.

LEARN TO RIDE